DISCOVERING BUGS

Kelly Gauthier
Introduction by Darlyne Murawski
Illustrated by Julius Csotonyi

APPLESAUCE PRESS

KENNEBUNKPORT, MAINE

13-Digit ISBN: 9781604336894
10-Digit ISBN: 1604336897

This book may be ordered by mail from the publisher. Please include $5.99 for postage and handling.
Please support your local bookseller first!

Books published by Cider Mill Press Book Publishers are available at special discounts for bulk purchases in the United States by corporations, institutions, and other organizations.
For more information, please contact the publisher.

Applesauce Press is an imprint of
Cider Mill Press Book Publishers
"Where good books are ready for press"
PO Box 454
12 Spring Street
Kennebunkport, Maine 04046

Visit us on the Web! www.cidermillpress.com

Cover and interior design by Alicia Freile, Tango Media
Typography: Gipsiero, Destroy, Imperfect, PMN Caecilia
All illustrations by Julius Csotonyi.
Vectors and borders used under official license by Shutterstock.com

Printed in China

2 3 4 5 6 7 8 9 0

TABLE OF CONTENTS

INTRODUCTION

Darlyne Murawski, author of *The Ultimate Bugopedia*

WHAT IS A "BUG?"

What does the word "bug" mean to you? We often refer to a small critter or "creepy crawly" as a bug. But the word has many meanings. There are "true bugs" – insects that scientists place in the order Hemiptera. If you get sick, you might have "caught a bug" – a virus or bacterium. If someone "bugs" you, that person is being annoying. A bug can also be a listening device to record conversations secretly. So, let's get specific.

In this book, we use the term "bug" to mean any **arthropod** – or small animal with jointed legs, a segmented body, and a hard exoskeleton. That includes the following:

● insects
● crustaceans (crabs, lobsters, shrimp, barnacles, wood lice, whale lice, and related species)
● myriapods (millipedes and centipedes) and
● chelicerates (spiders, scorpions, sea spiders, and horseshoe crabs – to name a few).

Bugs are found the world over, on all continents, from the warm tropics to the frigid polar regions, and from coastal shores to the deep sea. They may be small, but they rule the earth with their spectacular diversity. About 84% of all animals are arthropods! That includes more than a million named species of insects alone, and many more species await scientific description.

PARTS OF A BUG

Arthropods have either two or three body sections. Most have three: a head, a thorax, and an abdomen. Spiders, scorpions, ticks, and horseshoe crabs have two sections: a fused head and thorax, called a **cephalothorax**, and an abdomen.

Arthropods pump blood from their heart into open body cavities where their internal organs and tissues get bathed in blood. This open circulatory system is different from the closed system of arteries and veins that we have.

Early arthropods could see with **compound eyes** made up of many facets that work together to form a picture. This gave them the advantage of seeing more detail than could be seen with **simple eyes**. Today's arthropods have either compound or simple eyes, and some – like many insects – have both types. If you take a look at a grasshopper or a cicada, it has two large compound eyes, and in between them, three tiny simple eyes. By comparison, all spiders have simple eyes.

A rigid **exoskeleton** (external skeleton) supports an arthropod's body and protects it from predators and dehydration. Unlike the smooth, gradual growth of **vertebrates**, arthropods are **invertebrates** that grow in stages by molting, or shedding, their outer shell. The newly molted animal is soft-bodied at first until it expands in size and the cuticle gradually hardens. The thin exoskeleton left behind by a newly-shed arthropod looks like an empty shell of its former self.

For arthropods, growing up means not only shedding their own exterior but also changing body form. This change is called **metamorphosis**. Think of how a butterfly advances from caterpillar (**larva**) to **pupa**, to winged adult. This progression is called **complete metamorphosis**. Crabs, beetles, flies, and ants likewise hatch from the egg as tiny larvae and will change dramatically as they age. A simpler form of metamorphosis happens in some bugs such as grasshoppers, true bugs, scorpions, and spiders. The immature stage, the **nymph**, looks much like the adult in form.

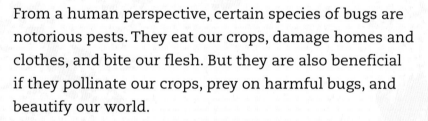

BUGS AND HUMANS

From a human perspective, certain species of bugs are notorious pests. They eat our crops, damage homes and clothes, and bite our flesh. But they are also beneficial if they pollinate our crops, prey on harmful bugs, and beautify our world.

BUGS IN NATURE

In nature, bugs serve many roles including as pollinators, decomposers and recyclers, and producers of silk, honey, beeswax, royal jelly, dyes, shellac, honeydew, and various medicines. Bugs can be herbivores, carnivores, or fungivores, depending on whether they eat plants, meat, or fungi, respectively.

Bugs are a large part of the food chain – serving as both predator and prey. Many birds, lizards, and other larger animals could not survive without bugs to feed on. Some bugs, like ticks and fleas, are **parasites** that feed on another creature — its host. Parasites do not kill their hosts; however, they may weaken them. But there is also a deadly form of parasite called a **parasitoid**. Parasitoids grow up feeding on their host, and in the process, slowly kill it – like cicada wasps do to cicadas, or like tarantula wasps do to tarantulas.

THE PAST AND FUTURE OF BUGS

Scientists have unearthed an incredible variety of ancient arthropod fossils from the Cambrian Period (540 to 490 million years ago). Some of the early arthropods to occupy the oceans included trilobites, sea scorpions, shellfish, and horseshoe crabs. Sea scorpions died out about 251 million years ago, and trilobites became extinct during the Jurassic period, about 200 million years ago.

Do bugs face extinction now? Some species are more vulnerable to extinction than others. Some die out due to the loss or damage of their natural habitat. Many species depend on one type of plant or one type of prey. They can be more vulnerable to extinction than others. Unfortunately, many arthropods are disappearing before scientists even have a chance to name them!

Knowledge is an important tool for us to make a difference in our world. Scientific research continues to provide information on the history, biology, and behavior of arthropods, but we can also learn so much just from simple observation. Bugs play an enormous part in the diversity of life on earth, and diversity is the key to maintaining the balance of life as we know it.

FEATHER-TAIL CENTIPEDE
(ALIPES GRANDIDIERI)

WHERE: Eastern Africa

SIZE: 10-15 centimeters (4-6 inches)

LOOK FOR: Two long legs on the end of the body that look like feathers or flags at the tips

BUG BITE: The feather-like legs on the back of this bug aren't just for show. When the feather-tail centipede is threatened, it shakes its back legs to make a hissing noise, like a rattlesnake. This centipede can also use its back legs to bite or pinch as defense against predators.

When a female feather-tail centipede lays eggs, she will protect the newly hatched centipedes by wagging her back legs to distract an approaching predator. Sometimes, the back section of her body will break off when she does this.

CREEPY CRAWLIES

Not all bugs need to fly. Some rely on dozens, or even hundreds, of legs to move around. Some burrow deep into the ground, and some will live high up in the trees. From the caves of South America to the oceans of Australia, there are hundreds of different types of bugs that crawl, scuttle, wriggle, and squirm.

From centipedes to spiders, these are the creepiest crawlers around!

GIANT CENTIPEDE

(SCOLOPENDRA GIGANTEA)

WHERE: South America and the Caribbean

SIZE: 26-30 centimeters (10-12 inches)

LOOK FOR: Long, slender body with lots of legs

BUG BITE: Much like its more common relative, the giant centipede has dozens of legs running along its body. The giant centipede is the largest of all centipedes and can reach up to 12 inches in length. Centipedes are venomous, and while their venom is not often dangerous to humans, it makes them a vicious predator.

The giant centipede is a carnivore, and its size allows it to prey on insects as well as other animals, such as lizards, frogs, small birds, mice, and even bats. The centipede then uses its venom to capture its prey.

The giant centipede will crawl to the ceiling of caves, hang from its back sets of legs, and wait for a passing bat to get close enough to catch.

9

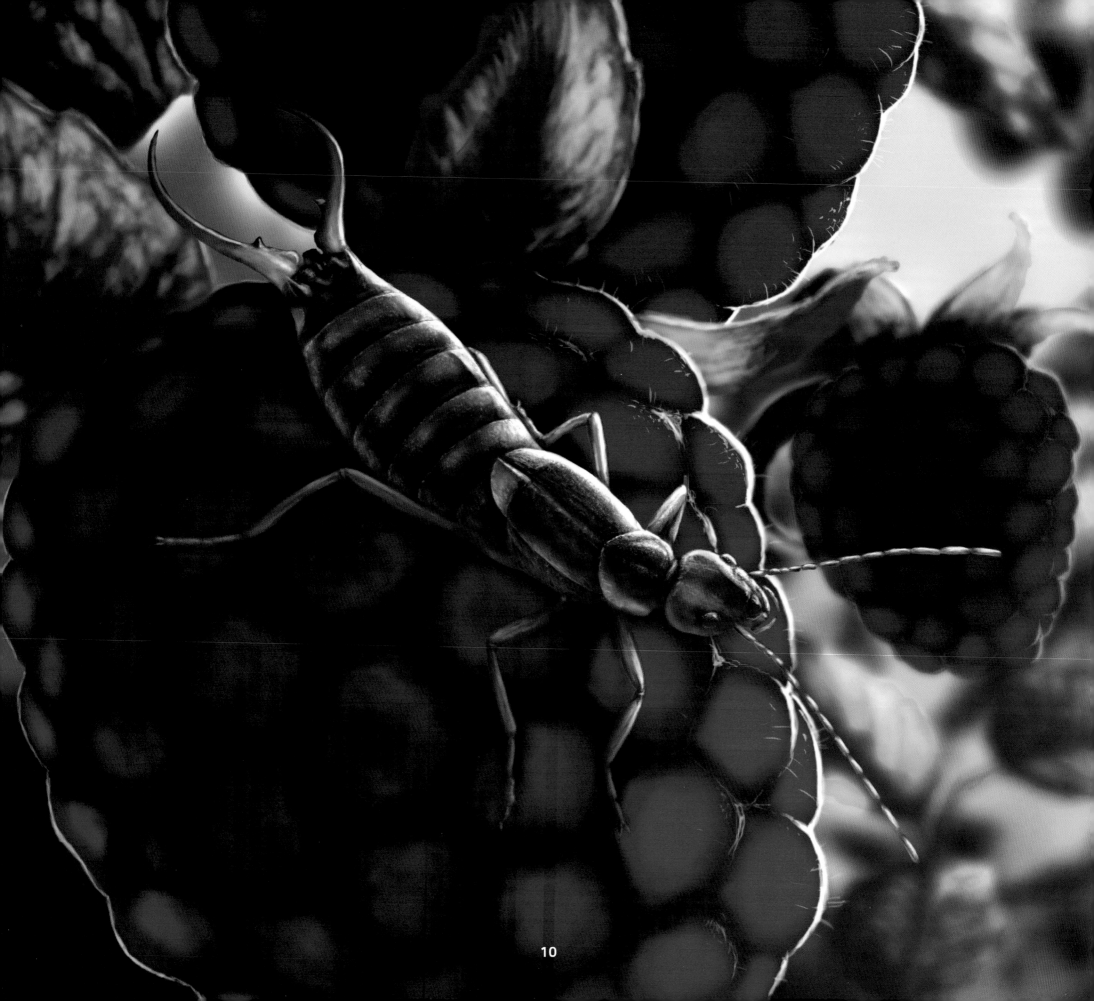

COMMON EUROPEAN EARWIG
(*FORFICULA AURICULARIA*)

WHERE: North America, Europe, and western Asia

SIZE: 12–20 millimeters (about ½ inch)

LOOK FOR: Reddish-brown color, flat body, and "pincers" on the end of the body

BUG BITE: Despite the name, earwigs don't live in ears. In fact, they can live in a wide variety of environments and are found in many different parts of the world. These distinctive little insects have pincers at the end of their bodies, and the males generally have larger and more curved pincers than the females. Although they can fly, common earwigs rarely do.

These bugs can be a real pest. They mostly come out at night and take shelter in dark, damp places. They can be very invasive if they take up residence in a house and will get into everything including floorboards, household plants, pantries, and even furniture and clothing.

This bug is classified as "invasive" in North America and Australia.

PEACOCK MITE
(TUCKERELLA JAPONICA)

WHERE: Tropical climates

SIZE: ½ millimeter

LOOK FOR: Orange body, leaf-like appendages on the body, and long hairs on the end of the body

BUG BITE: These tiny bugs are too small to see well with the naked eye. Their name comes from the leaf-like parts all over their backs, which resemble the tail of a peacock. They have tails of long hair on the back of their body that are used like whips to fight off predators. These mites are herbivores and prefer to live in warmer evironments where they can feed on grasses or citrus fruits.

ANTLION
(EUROLEON NOSTRAS)

WHERE: All over the world, but prefer warmer climates

SIZE: 12-15 centimeter (4½-6 inch) wingspan

LOOK FOR: Two pairs of narrow wings (similar to a dragonfly) in adults, small body with three pairs of legs and pincers at the head in larvae

BUG BITE: These bugs have a four-stage life cycle from egg to larva (young) to cocoon to adult. While the adult antlion is nocturnal and very similar to a dragonfly, the larva antlion is a ferocious bug. The young antlions are ambush predators and will conceal themselves in a funnel-like pit and wait for prey, particularly ants, to fall in.

The antlion larva is also sometimes called the "doodlebug," because the way it travels leaves a winding trail.

An ant (left) falls into the pit of the antlion larva (right).

GOOTY SAPPHIRE TARANTULA
(*POECILOTHERIA METALLICA*)

WHERE: Central and southern India

SIZE: 15-20 centimeters (6-8 inch) legspan

LOOK FOR: Bright blue color

BUG BITE: The name of this tarantula comes from the town where it was first discovered (Gooty), but it is sometimes known as the peacock or metallic tarantula as well. This tarantula is critically endangered because it lives only in one forest in India, and their habitat is getting smaller. These spiders are very defensive and live most often in holes of trees. They create funnel-like webs to catch their prey, and eat other insects as their main source of food. While males may only live for a few years, the females have a lifespan of up to twelve years!

Like other tarantulas, these spiders are venomous. The fangs of an adult can grow to be nearly ¾ inch, and the effects of their bite can be painful and dangerous.

GIANT PILL MILLIPEDE
(SPHAEROTHERIUM GIGANTEUM)

WHERE: Southern and southeast Asia, southern Africa, Australia

SIZE: 1-3 centimeters (1-3 inches)

LOOK FOR: Black body with red plates

BUG BITE: This bug has a great defense. The outer part of the giant pill millipede's body is hard for protection. When they feel threatened, these bugs roll up into a ball. The tail of the pill millipede wraps all the way around and covers its head, making a perfectly round armor. When rolled up, these giant bugs are typically about the same size as a golf ball, although some have been known to be as big as a baseball.

PYCNOGONID
COMMONLY KNOWN AS
SEA SPIDER
(*ANOPLODACTYLUS EVANSI*)

WHERE: Australia

SIZE: Body up to 1 centimeter

LOOK FOR: Red and blue body

BUG BITE: The sea spider is made up of more leg than body. This spider can swim, and moves best when carried by waves and the tide. Unlike land spiders, the sea spider does not create a web. Instead, this type of bug lives in rock pools and on coral reefs, where it hunts for food. They can even survive as far as 16 meters, or about 52 feet, under the sea. The colors of the sea spider help it to blend in with the reef around it to better hide from predators.

The sea spider is a predator that feeds on aquatic worms and slugs, and it uses claws on its front legs to capture prey.

EMPEROR SCORPION
(PANDINUS IMPERATOR)

WHERE: Western Africa

SIZE: 20 centimeters (8 inches)

LOOK FOR: Dark body, two front pincers, and a long, curved tail

BUG BITE: The emperor scorpion lives in both rainforests and savannas, where it burrows into the soil beneath rocks and leaves. The body of a scorpion is hard for protection and has a metallic shine. In fact, emperor scorpions will glow under ultraviolet light. Their curved tail has a special stinger filled with venom that helps the scorpion to paralyze its prey. Although they may look intimidating, these scorpions are fairly harmless to humans. A scorpion sting is similar to a bee sting. It may hurt, but it usually won't cause much of a reaction unless the victim is allergic to the venom.

Their front pincers aren't just for show;
they help this scorpion catch and hold
onto insects, mice, and lizards.

PEACOCK SPIDER
(MARATUS SPECIOSUS)

WHERE: Australia

SIZE: 3–5 millimeters (⅛ inch)

LOOK FOR: Fuzzy blue body with yellow and red markings

BUG BITE: The peacock spider lives exclusively in Australia and prefers the sand dunes of the coast. Although it is both tiny and colorful, this bug is most well-known for its dancing abilities. A type of jumping spider, the peacock spider has a unique mating dance in which it wiggles its body and raises and lowers its third pair of legs.

RUBY-TAILED WASP
(CHRYSIS IGNITA)

WHERE: Europe

SIZE: 10-12 millimeters (about ½ inch)

LOOK FOR: Metallic body, blue thorax, and red abdomen

BUG BITE: The ruby-tailed wasp is part of a family known as cuckoo wasps. This beautiful wasp is capable of curling up in a ball to protect itself. Its body has a hard shell around it to prevent stings from other types of wasps and bees. This type of wasp is known as a parasite. It will make its home in the nest of bees and will eat the eggs and larvae that live in the nest. Unlike other types of wasps, cuckoo wasps are incapable of stinging.

BUGS THAT TAKE FLIGHT!

From butterflies to bees, there are plenty of bugs that have mastered both land and sky. Most commonly, flying bugs will have either two or four wings. Insects like bees, wasps, moths, and butterflies all have two pairs of wings, or a total of four wings. Flies, on the other hand, only have one pair of wings. But be careful what you swat! Some of these bugs won't take too kindly to being whacked at.

You'll notice that some of the bugs in this section are caterpillars; they are still in a larva stage. While they can't fly yet, they will eventually turn into moths or butterflies with fully-developed wings.

Male orchid bees smell particularly good. They are very attracted to the scent of the orchids and will gather the oils from the flower so that they smell just as wonderful!

HANSON'S ORCHID BEE
(*EUGLOSSA HANSONI*)

WHERE: South America

SIZE: 1-2 centimeters

LOOK FOR: Metallic blue, green, copper, or gold body

BUG BITE: Orchid bees are named after their favorite food: the nectar of orchid flowers. This bee has an unusually long tongue that can reach into the orchid to eat the hidden nectar. The nectar gives them energy to fly a long way to their next flower, with some going miles away for their next meal. The orchid needs the bee just as the bee needs the orchid. These bees collect the pollen from one orchid and bring it to the next, helping the flowers stay alive.

CRIMSON MARSH GLIDER
(TRITHEMIS AURORA)

WHERE: Asia

SIZE: 2-3 centimeters (about 1 inch)

LOOK FOR: Bright red body in males; yellow or brown body with black lines in females

BUG BITE: The crimson marsh glider is a type of dragonfly. It is named for the color of the males, who have a bright red body and wings with dark spots. The females look very different, with yellow or brownish bodies. They have black lines along their body segments and dark spots on their wings. These dragonflies live mostly in marshes, ponds, or slow streams.

This crimson marsh glider hunts a mosquito. Mosquitos are well-known carriers of dangerous diseases like malaria.

MONARCH BUTTERFLY
(*DANAUS PLEXIPPUS*)

WHERE: North America and northern South America

SIZE: 8-12 centimeter (3-4 inches) wingspan

LOOK FOR: Orange wings with black lines and white spots

BUG BITE: The monarch butterfly is one of the most recognizable types of butterflies. It has a life cycle with four stages in it. The first stage of their life is the egg, which is laid on a milkweed plant. The eggs hatch into caterpillars just about four days after they are laid, and the caterpillars spend two weeks growing. Then, the caterpillar will use silk to create a chrysalis, or cocoon, where it changes into a butterfly. After about 10 days in the cocoon, the fully grown monarch butterfly emerges.

Monarch butterflies are most well-known for their migration. Every fall, the monarch butterflies migrate from their home in North America to South America to live out the winter months. Fascinatingly, the butterflies only live long enough to make the journey once in their lives, so it is unclear how the new butterflies know where to go each year.

A bird flies off in fear after being fooled by the caterpillar's snake impression.

SNAKE-MIMICKING CATERPILLAR
(*HEMEROPLANES TRIPTOLEMUS*)

WHERE: South America

SIZE: 1-10 centimeters (up to 4 inches) in length

LOOK FOR: Green or brown body, white spots that look like eyes

BUG BITE: At rest, this caterpillar looks completely normal. When threatened, it will twist and turn its body to reveal a patterned underside, pull in its legs, and puff up a section at the front of its body. The area it inflates has markings that look like eyes, and this caterpillar quickly begins to look like a small snake. In order to protect itself, this little caterpillar will twist and turn its body like a slithering snake, and will even strike out like a snake going after prey to scare off approaching predators.

TAILED EMPEROR BUTTERFLY CATERPILLAR
(POLYURA SEMPRONIUS)

WHERE: Australia

SIZE: About 5-8 centimeters (2-3 inches)

LOOK FOR: Green body with yellow lines and crescent-shaped markings, two pairs of horns on the head

BUG BITE: This caterpillar is unique for its interesting head horns, with two pairs on its head. The caterpillar is native to Australia and feeds mostly on local foliage. Fully mature, this caterpillar becomes the spectacular tailed emperor butterfly, which is quite large (about 7-8 centimeters) and known for being a fast, strong flyer.

VENEZUELAN POODLE MOTH
(ARTACE CRIBRARIA)

WHERE: Venezuela

SIZE: 2½-6 centimeter (up to 2 inches) wingspan

LOOK FOR: White wings, fluffy body

BUG BITE: This moth is part of a family of "dot-lined white moths," which can be found all over North America, but this particular type is native to Venezuela. Its body is even fluffier than those of its family, which led to it being named after a poodle because its hairs look almost like fur. Their hairs can help them sense their environment, and protect against certain predators. Like other moths, this one is nocturnal, and lives primarily in trees. Its larvae are brown and white in color and often look like twigs as a form of protection.

NYCTERIBIID BAT FLY
(PENICILLIDIA FULVIDA)

WHERE: Europe, North America, Africa, Asia, and Australia

SIZE: 1–5 millimeters

LOOK FOR: Brown, spider-like body

BUG BITE: This fly is sometimes called a bat fly, because they are parasites that attach onto bats. Unlike other flies, these bugs don't have any wings of their own. Instead, they attach onto a bat's face and live there for their entire life. The blood of their host bat is their main form of food.

A nycteribiid bat fly attached to the head of a horseshoe bat.

SPILOMYIA FLY
(SPILOMYIA LONGICORNIS)

WHERE: North America

SIZE: 10-15 millimeters (about ½ inch)

LOOK FOR: Black and yellow striped body, two wings

BUG BITE: This fly is great at pretending to be a bee. It will hover in the air or over flowers and make buzzing noises, and its yellow and black body looks like a wasp or yellow jacket. These flies eat mostly pollen and nectar. Although their bee imitation might fool predators into staying away, they cannot sting like bees can.

One way to distinguish these flies from bees is to look at their wings. Flies only have two wings, while bees have four.

YUCCA MOTH
(TEGETICULA YUCCASELLA)

WHERE: Southwestern United States and Mexico

SIZE: 2 – 3 centimeter (1 inch) wingspan

LOOK FOR: White or silvery wings

BUG BITE: The yucca moth lives in harmony with the yucca plant, and they could not exist without each other. The female moth's main job is to pollinate the yucca plant, and she will always lay eggs within the yucca flower. In return, the yucca flower is the only source of food for yucca moth larvae.

The yucca moth has a specially developed mouth that looks like tentacles, which helps it to collect and transport the yucca flower's pollen from plant to plant. This process only happens at night.

A female yucca moth pollinates a yucca flower in the moonlight.

A tiger beetle catches and eats a small bee.

TIGER BEETLE
(*CICINDELA AURULENTA*)

WHERE: China, Thailand, and Malaysia

SIZE: 16-18 millimeters (about ½ inch)

LOOK FOR: Blue body with red stripe and white or yellow spots

BUG BITE: This beetle is sometimes referred to as the golden-spotted tiger beetle, in reference to its trademark yellowish spots. Tiger beetles are known for being fierce predators because of their strong pincer-like mouths and their speed. Tiger beetles are incredibly fast runners. Sometimes they run so quickly that they can't see and have to stop when in pursuit of their prey in order to get their bearings.

BEETLES, WEEVILS, AND ANTS

Beetles are easily recognized by their hard exoskeletons, and they have cases covering their wings called elytra. Most beetles have two elytra that meet in the center of their body, and they will open them up to fly. Some beetles have only one hard case covering their body, making them flightless. Weevils are types of beetles with similar body structures, but what really sets these bugs apart is their long snout. Weevils are known for being pests because they eat plants and can destroy crops such as grain and cotton.

Ants, like beetles and weevils, are a type of insect with an exoskeleton. Ants have a very interesting lifestyle. They typically live in large colonies, with worker or soldier ants helping to support the colony, which is led by a queen.

TRILOBITE BEETLE
(PLATERODRILUS PARADOXUS)

WHERE: India, Southeast Asia, and other tropical areas

SIZE: 40-60 millimeters (females), 5-8 millimeters (males)

LOOK FOR: Black body with orange spines

BUG BITE: The female form of this beetle is particularly interesting because she stays in larvae form for her whole life and looks very different from the males. While male trilobite beetles look a lot like many other beetles, the females get much larger and grow into long, black bodies with orange spines along their sides. Most of these beetles will eat the fungi found in their tropical habitats.

RAINBOW DUNG BEETLE
(PHANAEUS VINDEX)

WHERE: North America

SIZE: 1–2 centimeters

LOOK FOR: Metallic green, yellow, and red body

BUG BITE: The rainbow dung beetle is named for the rainbow of colors covering its body. It is part of a family of bugs called scarab beetles, which used to be worshiped in ancient Egypt. The males have a large horn on the front of their head. The "dung" part of the beetle's name comes from where it is born. This beetle will tunnel under a pile of dung to lay their eggs.

POLKA-DOTTED CLOWN WEEVIL

(PACHYRRHYNCHUS ORBIFER)

WHERE: Phillippines

SIZE: 6-8 millimeters

LOOK FOR: Black body with metallic blue and orange spots

BUG BITE: This brilliantly-colored weevil is named after a clown for its noticeable polka dots. The spots are made up of tons of tiny spots, giving this weevil the appearance of being covered in glitter. These weevils are rare and are sought after by bug collectors for their unique appearance.

GOLIATH BEETLE
(GOLIATHUS GOLIATUS)

WHERE: Africa

SIZE: 5-10 centimeters (2-4 inches)

LOOK FOR: Dark brown body, black head with white stripes

BUG BITE: This large beetle is named after the biblical Goliath for its size. The Goliath beetle is one of the largest types of beetles, and can sometimes grow to be as large as a small bird. These beetles have a pair of wings that stay tucked underneath their body until they need to travel. Male Goliath beetles have a Y-shaped horn at the end of their heads. Most often, they use this horn to fight with other Goliath beetles over food or mates.

The Goliath beetle typically lives in forest or savanna areas, so its main food is tree sap and fruit common to its habitat.

RED DRIVER ANT
(DORYLUS HELVOLUS)

WHERE: Africa and tropical parts of Asia

SIZE: 2-8 millimeters in length

LOOK FOR: Reddish body, large head, pincers

BUG BITE: The driver ant lives in colonies that can have millions of ants living together in one anthill. When these ants need to scavenge for food, they will move out in an army, with millions of ants forming one long column. Some of these ants are "soldier" ants. They have larger heads than the normal driver ants and incredibly powerful pincers. These ants will protect the boundaries of their army by attacking any threats with their pincers. These ants can bite and sting, and when they do it can be painful.

A smaller driver ant uses a larger
soldier ant for protection.

BLACK BULLDOG ANT
(MYRMECIA PYRIFORMIS)

WHERE: Australia

SIZE: About 2 centimeters

LOOK FOR: Dark red or brownish body, front pincers

BUG BITE: This bug has been classified by the Guinness World Records as the world's most dangerous ant! This bug was named for its determination in a fight—it definitely won't give up when attacked. With both front pincers and a back stinger, the bulldog ant can fight from all angles and will often grab an attacker with its pincers, swing its lower body around, and sting at the same time. It can sting multiple times in a row very quickly, giving it a big advantage in a fight. This tiny bug isn't afraid of humans, and there have been recorded deaths from too many bulldog ant stings.

A bulldog ant (right) battles a wasp. Because both can sting, this fight may seem evenly matched, but the bulldog ant's strong pincers give it an advantage.

GIRAFFE WEEVIL
(TRACHELOPHORUS GIRAFFA)

WHERE: Madagascar

SIZE: About 2 centimeters

LOOK FOR: Red body, long black neck

BUG BITE: This weevil is named after the animal it resembles, with a long neck that gives it a giraffe-like appearance. A male's neck can be two or three times longer than a female's. Their long necks are mostly used to help them in fighting and building nests. When a female gets ready to lay an egg, she will find a small tree, roll one of the leaves into a tube, and lay her eggs within the tube for protection.

FROG-LEGGED BEETLE

(SAGRA BUQUETI)

WHERE: Southeast Asia

SIZE: 25–50 millimeters (1-2 inches)

LOOK FOR: Metallic green body, large hind legs in males

BUG BITE: Unsurprisingly, this beetle is named for a frog because of the large, frog-like legs of the male beetles. Their large hind legs certainly help them cling to branches, but they also help them win wrestling matches against other males. The beetle will sometimes wiggle his back legs at another beetle in threat of an attack.

HERCULES BEETLE
(DYNASTES HERCULES)

WHERE: Central and South America

SIZE: Males up to 18 centimeters, females up to 7 centimeters

LOOK FOR: Yellow body, large black horn in males

BUG BITE: The Hercules beetle is named after the ancient Greek figure for its impressive size and strength. In fact, it is the third largest beetle known. This beetle is characterized as a rhinocerous beetle beause of the large black horn on the males. These horns allow them to carry food and objects that are eighty times heavier than the beetle itself.

This beetle only lives as an adult for a few months, but it will remain in its larval stage for up to two years, surviving mainly on rotting wood. It is capable of flying, but is more likely to be found on the mossy ground of the forest, hunting for fallen fruit or leaves to eat.

A Hercules beetle rests on the moss next to a poison dart frog.

SPINY FLOWER MANTIS

(PSEUDOCREOBOTRA WAHLBERGII)

WHERE: Southern and eastern Africa

SIZE: 3–5 centimeters (1-2 inches)

LOOK FOR: Beige body with green and orange or brown markings in a swirl pattern

BUG BITE: Like other mantis bugs, the spiny flower mantis uses its body as camouflage to pretend to be a flower to lure prey, but what makes this mantis unique is how it responds to predators. When a threat approaches, this mantis raises its wings to show the spiral markings, which look like large eyes. This defense startles the predator, and tricks it into believing the mantis is much larger than it really is.

CLASSIC AND COOL

You may recognize some of these bugs right away as backyard residents. From the lightning bug to the ladybeetle, these bugs are easy to spot because they are so common. But some of these bugs might be difficult to spot at all! Because insects are so small, they have to become masters of camouflage. From pretending to be a flower to looking like a leaf, these bugs can hide in plain sight.

DEVIL'S FLOWER MANTIS
(IDOLOMANTIS DIABOLICA)

WHERE: Africa

SIZE: 10-13 centimeters (3–5 inches)

LOOK FOR: Brown or green body, large front legs

BUG BITE: The devil's flower mantis is named for its ability to pretend to be a flower. As a predator, it perches on the leaf or branch and blends into the green and brown of the flower. The mantis will remain absolutely motionless, imitating a flower, until its prey tries to land. Then, the mantis will strike and grab onto its prey. This allows it to feed on other airborne insects that would be too hard to catch while it flies.

When threatened, the devil's flower mantis will raise its front legs to show red, white, blue, purple, or black markings beneath and quickly move its vibrantly colored wings to confuse or frighten predators.

MOSS MIMIC STICK INSECT

(TRYCHOPEPLUS LACINIATUS)

WHERE: Costa Rica and other tropical regions

SIZE: 4-8 centimeters (about 2-3 inches)

LOOK FOR: Long, slender body with brown and green tufts

BUG BITE: Don't be fooled—this is no stick! Also known as a "walking stick," this tropical insect has a unique type of camouflage that makes it look covered in moss, so it blends into the trees and moss of its tropical habitat. When it stays still, the stick insect looks so much like moss that it is almost invisible. This camouflage makes a great defense against predators in the jungle, keeping this herbivore insect safe in the trees.

BROAD-WINGED KATYDID

(MICROCENTRUM RHOMBIFOLIUM)

WHERE: Southwestern and eastern United States (excluding New England)

SIZE: 5-6 centimeters (about 2 inches)

LOOK FOR: Wide, green wings

BUG BITE: The katydid likes shady areas, and is often found in forests or areas with lots of leaves and shrubs. As a disguise, the katydid's green wings are angled and covered in veins, which makes them look like a small leaf. You might hear this bug before you see it. The katydid has a very recognizable call that sounds like a repeated ticking noise and lasts for a few seconds at a time.

HARLEQUIN LADYBEETLE
(HARMONIA AXYRIDIS)

WHERE: Asia, North America, South America, Europe, South Africa

SIZE: 5½ – 8 ½ millimeters

LOOK FOR: Red body with black spots

BUG BITE: The harlequin ladybeetle is more commonly known as a "ladybug." The markings on the ladybeetle can vary. Ladybeetles can be very helpful in the wild because they feed on bugs known as plant lice, which can be harmful to plants and crops. But, these beetles can also become a problem for houses. Because they don't like the cold months, ladybeetles often invade homes in the winter. Like other beetles, they will release a smell and fluid when frightened or threatened to scare off predators. Ladybeetles are said to be good luck.

LIGHTNING BUG

(PHOTINUS PYRALIS)

WHERE: North America

SIZE: 10-15 millimeters

LOOK FOR: Red head, black body, and yellow or "lit" tail area

BUG BITE: Another common name for this bug is the "firefly," and if you've ever seen it at night you know why. Though it can be known as a fly, this bug is actually a type of beetle. They are most easily spotted as the sun is going down, when they use a special organ on the lower part of their body to flash light patterns. These patterns of light help the lightning bugs to find one another at night. However, their lights can also attract predators, so lightning bugs need to have a great defense. To protect themselves, lightning bugs will release a bad smell or a sticky substance when a predator attacks.

LEICHHARDT'S GRASSHOPPER

(PETASIDA EPHIPPIGERA)

WHERE: Australia

SIZE: 5-7 centimeters (2–2½ inches)

LOOK FOR: Orange body with blue and black spots

BUG BITE: These grasshoppers prefer to eat a minty-smelling, but bitter-tasting, plant called pityrodia, and will often live on just one bush for their entire lives. Thanks to the bitter taste of the pityrodia bush, these grasshoppers taste terrible, so they are less likely to become prey!

A brilliantly colored
Leichhardt's grasshopper
rests on a pityrodia plant.

ROOSTER TAIL CICADA
(LYSTRA LANATA)

WHERE: Tropical regions, particularly in South America

SIZE: 2-3 centimeters (about 1 inch)

LOOK FOR: Black speckled body, long fringe-like tail

BUG BITE: This insect gets its name from its spectacular tail, which has a feather-like appearance. This tail is used to distract approaching predators, and may even trick them into attacking the moving tail, allowing the insect to escape unharmed. The rooster tail cicada is closely related to other types of cicada bugs. It lives mostly in tropical regions, where it feeds on the sap of trees.

RED-AND-BLACK STRIPED STINK BUG
(GRAPHOSOMA LINEATUM)

WHERE: Parts of Europe, Western Asia, and North Africa

SIZE: 8-12 millimeters

LOOK FOR: Red and black stripes on the body

BUG BITE: This bug is also known as a type of shield bug, because the striped section of their body acts as a shield to protect them from predators. Their colors act as a warning to oncoming predators as well, because these bugs do not taste good. That's why they are called stink bugs. The striped stink bug prefers dry climates and will hide in trees when the weather is bad.

SPINY ORB-WEAVER
(GASTERACANTHA ARCUATA)

WHERE: Southeast Asia

SIZE: About 1 centimeter

LOOK FOR: Small orange body with three large spines

BUG BITE: The spiny orb-weaver is a type of spider with large spines that nearly triple its body size (they can be up to 3 centimeters end to end). These spines help protect this small spider from predators. The orb-weaver's web is recognizable for its web shape, which looks like a wheel. Once their web is built, the orb-weaver can wait for prey to come to them rather than having to go out and hunt for food.

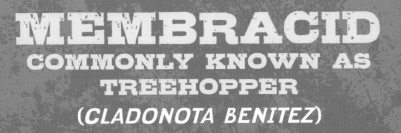

MEMBRACID
COMMONLY KNOWN AS TREEHOPPER
(*CLADONOTA BENITEZ*)

WHERE: South America

SIZE: 2-20 millimeters

LOOK FOR: Crescent-shaped body

BUG BITE: This bug is best known for its strange shape. In fact, it barely looks like a bug at all! This bug's crescent shape and forest-y colors help it to camouflage into its habitat. This type of bug is part of a family known as "tree hoppers," because of the way that it hops between trees in the forest.

STRANGEST SHAPE

SUPERLATIVES

Each of the bugs featured in this section has something special that sets them apart from the thousands of other types of bugs. Some are distinct because of their shape, like the giant coconut crab and the tiny fairyfly. Some are interesting for their looks, like the Elvis Presley shield bug. Some are exciting for their skills, like the creative defense of the assassin bug.

Big or small, furry or tough, flying or crawling, these bugs come in all shapes and sizes, with an endless variety. These section includes the most unique bugs known to mankind!

COCONUT CRAB
(BIRGUS LATRO)

WHERE: Tropical islands in the Indian and Pacific Oceans

SIZE: Up to 1 meter (about 3 feet)

LOOK FOR: Brown body, oversized front claws

BUG BITE: Like its relatives the scorpion and the ant, this bug has a hard outer body when it is fully grown. This bug is not a fan of humans and prefers to live on islands that are not crowded with people. The coconut crab has good reason not to trust humans—this bug is considered a delicacy in some places, and is sometimes considered a protected species in areas where it has been over-hunted. Young coconut crabs are similar to hermit crabs, and will find an empty shell on the beach to protect their backs until they are able to grow their own shells.

Unlike other types of crabs, the coconut crab lives primarily on land, in burrows under the sand. These crabs do need some contact with water, especially when it is time to lay eggs, and will usually live within a few miles of the ocean. During the day, coconut crabs usually stay tucked away in their burrows, and come out at night to hunt for food. This habit has led to some people calling this bug the "robber crab."

LARGEST BUG

As its name suggests, a favored food of the coconut crab is the coconut, and it has even been known to climb up palm trees in search of their favorite treat. At the top of the tree, the crab will drop the coconut to the ground to break it open.

71

ELVIS PRESLEY SHIELD BUG
(*PENTATOMOIDEA*)

WHERE: Southeast Asia

SIZE: 5-18 millimeters (about ½ inch)

LOOK FOR: Yellow body with black, blue, and white markings

BUG BITE: This bug looks like it's ready to rock and roll! This rare giant shield bug is a type of stink bug that sprays a bad-smelling liquid from its body when threatened to help fight off predators. The black markings on its back have led to the Elvis Presley nickname, because it looks like it has eyes, a nose, and the king's trademark hairdo. Others have said that this bug looks like the *Sesame Street* character Bert.

CELEBRITY LOOK-ALIKE

GIANT ATLAS MOTH

(ATTACUS ATLAS)

WHERE: Southeast Asia

SIZE: Wingspan about 25-30 centimeters (10-12 inches)

LOOK FOR: Large, reddish-brown wings with white markings

BUG BITE: These moths have a huge wingspan, and the overall size of their body is enormous for a bug! The name Atlas dates all the way back to Ancient Greece and can have a few meanings. The Greek god Atlas was known for his size and strength, so the moth's name could be a reference to its size. Some people say that atlas refers to the map-like markings of the moth's wings, because atlases are collections of maps. Or, the name could be a reference to the Cantonese translation, which means "snake's head moth." The tips of this moth's wings do look like the head of a snake!

The Atlas moth is treasured for the silk that it produces, and its large cocoon is very durable. In some places, the cocoons can be made into change purses if they stay intact.

ASSASSIN BUG

(*ACANTHASPIS PETAX*)

BEST DEFENSE

WHERE: East Africa and Malaysia

SIZE: About 1 centimeter (½ inch)

LOOK FOR: Black mound on body, similar in shape to the shell of a hermit crab

BUG BITE: This bug is one fierce hunter, and it likes to show off its prey. The assassin bug hunts ants as food, but then uses sticky saliva to add the ant corpse to the mound of bodies on its back. Scientists think that the assassin bug uses this deadly disguise to trick predators. By making its body look larger and differently shaped with the ant mound, the assassin bug is unrecognizable to the spiders that would normally try to hunt it.

LANTERN BUG
(*PYROPS INTRICATA*)

WHERE: Southeast Asia

SIZE: 6-8 centimeters (about 3 inches)

LOOK FOR: Green spotted or striped wings, long red "horn"

BUG BITE: This bug may look like it has a horn, but the long, red part of its head is actually a very long mouth, allowing it to better get into plants and trees to find food. Its mouth is often about half of its overall body size. This type of bug is part of a family called "planthoppers," because of their ability to hop between plants. Sadly, the lantern fly does not actually light up. It likely got its name because its wing are reflective, but it does not produce light.

NORTHERN MOLE CRICKET
(NEOCURTILLA HEXADACTYLA)

WHERE: Eastern North America

SIZE: 2-3 centimeters (about 1 inch)

LOOK FOR: Brown, hard body

BUG BITE: The front legs of the mole cricket are flattened and adapted for burrowing. Much like the mole it is named for, the mole cricket will burrow deep into muddy ground near lakes and streams. These crickets have a low-pitched chirp and will call from their burrows. As protection, the mole cricket is able to release a slimy substance to fight off predators.

BEST BURROWER

WASP MANTIDFLY
(CLIMACIELLA BRUNNEA)

WHERE: North America

SIZE: 2-3 centimeters (about 1 inch)

LOOK FOR: Black body with yellow stripes

BUG BITE: This bug may look like a wasp with its black and yellow body, but this appearance is a disguise. This bug is a predator and uses the fact that it looks like a wasp to its advantage. The wasp mantidfly hovers around flowers to set its trap. When another bug mistakes it for a wasp and gets too close, the mantidfly uses its front two legs to snatch its prey out of the air.

WEAVER ANT-MIMICKING JUMPING SPIDER

(MYRMARACHNE SMARAGDINA)

WHERE: Australia

SIZE: 5-6 millimeters (¼ inch)

LOOK FOR: Green body, similar shape and size to an ant

BUG BITE: This jumping spider doesn't look much like a spider at all. That's because this bug is another type of mimicking bug. The spider looks incredibly similar to a weaver ant. The biggest difference between the two is how many legs they have. Weaver ants only have six legs, but the mimicking spider has eight. So, the spider will raise its front two legs to create fake antennae to complete the disguise. The spider will live in close proximity to weaver ant colonies and will pretend to be part of the colony to look for prey.

BEST DISGUISE

On the left is a weaver ant, but on the right is the weaver ant-mimicking jumping spider.

FAIRYFLY WASP
(KIKIKI HUNA)

WHERE: Tropical areas such as Hawaii, Costa Rica, and Trinidad

SIZE: Less than 1/5 millimeter

LOOK FOR: Black, yellow, or brown colored body

BUG BITE: This bug is so small that it is very rarely spotted by humans. This little wasp has a lifespan of only a few days. Though not much is known about this small but mighty bug, it has been around for thousands of years. In fact, fossils of fairyfly relatives have been found from prehistoric eras.

SMALLEST FLYNG INSECT

Two tiny fairyfly wasps rest on a leaf while a honey bee (usually about 1 centimeter in size) drinks water in the background. A Paramecium (which grow to be ¼ inch) swims inside a water droplet.

INDEX

About the Introduction Writer

Darlyne Murawski, PhD is a lifelong bug lover, with a doctorate degree in Biology from the University of Texas and experience as a research biologist and nature photographer. She has written buggish articles for National Geographic Magazine and several books and articles on these critters, including *The Ultimate Bugopedia* (with Nancy Honovich), *Bug Faces, Face to Face with Butterflies*, and *Spiders and Their Webs*.

About the Author

Kelly Gauthier is a writer, researcher, editor, and enthusiast of animals big and small. Her love of bugs started at a young age with a bug-collecting kit, which sent her to the backyard to collect caterpillars, worms, and "roly-poly" bugs, and she is incredibly grateful to her parents for always indulging her butterfly obsession. When she doesn't have her nose buried in a book, she is most likely to be found talking about bugs with the talented team at Cider Mill Press (especially publisher John Whalen, Brittany Wason, and Deana Coddaire). She is based in New England.

About the Illustrator

Julius Csotonyi is one of the world's most high-profile and talented contemporary scientific illustrators. His considerable academic expertise informs his stunning, dynamic art. He has created life-sized dinosaur murals for the Royal Ontario Museum and for the Dinosaur Hall at the Natural History Museum of Los Angeles County as well as most of the artwork for the new Hall of Paleontology at the Houston Museum of Natural Science. He lives in Canada.

His books include *Discovering Sharks*, *The T. Rex Handbook*, *The Paleoart of Julius Csotonyi*, and *Prehistoric Predators*.

About Applesauce Press

Good ideas ripen with time. From seed to harvest, Applesauce Press crafts books with beautiful designs, creative formats, and kid-friendly information on a variety of fascinating topics. Like our parent company, Cider Mill Press Book Publishers, our press bears fruit twice a year, publishing a new crop of titles each spring and fall.

KENNEBUNKPORT, MAINE

Write to us at:

PO Box 454
Kennebunkport, ME 04046

Or visit us on the web at:
www.cidermillpress.com